THE ILLUSTRATED HISTORY OF
LAS VEGAS

THE ILLUSTRATED HISTORY OF
LAS VEGAS

GENERAL EDITOR:

DAVID JACK CANNON

CHARTWELL
BOOKS, INC.

This edition published in 1997 by
CHARTWELL BOOKS, INC.
A Division of BOOKSALES, INC
PO Box 7100
114 Northfield Avenue, Edison
New Jersey 08818-7100

Produced by the
Promotional Reprint Company Ltd,
Kiln House, 210 New Kings Road, London SW6 4NZ

Design © 1997 American Graphic Systems, Inc.

Designed and captioned by Bill Yenne, with design assistance from Azia Yenne
and proofreading by Andy Roe and Joan B. Hayes.

ISBN 0 7858 0831 0

Printed and bound in China

Picture Credits:
With the exceptions listed below, all of the pictures in this book were supplied
through the courtesy of the property pictured and/or mentioned in the caption.

AGS Archives: Pages 9, 11, 12, 13, 16, 17, 18, 73.
Binion's Horseshoe Hotel & Casino: Page 169.
David Bolzano Hollywood Images: Pages 44-45, 47, 55, 58-59, 64-65, 68-69, 74, 75, 76-77, 81, 82 bottom, 140-141.
Eddie Brandt's Saturday Matinee: 68 top, 68 bottom.
Excalibur Hotel & Casino: Pages 108, 108-109, 110-111, 111, 112, 113, 178.
Golden Gate Hotel & Casino: Page 14.
Lady Luck Hotel & Casino: Pages 1, 2, 7 top, 7 bottom, 80 top, 80 bottom, 88, 126, 135, 172, 175.
Las Vegas Hilton: Pages 76, 78, 79, 84, 85, 130, 130-131, 168.
Las Vegas News Bureau: Pages 32-33, 42, 48-49, 56-57, 62-63, 66-67.
Luxor Hotel & Casino: Pages 146, 150.
© M.J. McPike: Page 30.
Mirage Resorts: Pages 91, 94-95, 96, 97, 98, 100, 188-189.
Nevada Commission on Tourism: Pages 104, 107 top, 107 bottom, 176.

New York New York Hotel & Casino: Pages 164, 165, 166-167.
Riviera Hotel & Casino: Pages 39, 46, 51, 136, 137.
Showboat Hotel & Casino: Pages 54, 58, 82 top, 83, 125, 132, 140.
Treasure Island at the Mirage: Pages 114, 115, 116, 117, 118, 119.
University of Nevada Las Vegas: Pages 18-19, 20-21, 22-23, 28, 29, 30-31, 34-35, 36-37, 40-41, 43, 52-53, 70-71, 92-93.
United States Bureau of Reclamation: Pages 25, 26 top, 26 bottom, 26-27.
© Bill Yenne: Pages 6-7, 10, 15, 50, 60-61, 61, 86, 87, 88-89, 99, 101, 102-103, 105, 106, 120, 121, 122, 122-123, 126-127, 128 top, 128 bottom, 129, 133, 134-135, 138, 138-139, 142-143, 145, 146-147, 148, 148-149, 150-151, 152, 153, 154-155, 156, 157, 158, 159, 160, 161, 162-163, 170-171, 172-173, 174-175, 176-177, 178-179, 180-181, 181, 182-183, 184-185, 186-187, 192, covers.

Contents

ABOVE: An enthusiastic Keno winner strikes green at the Lady Luck Casino (top), while lucky sevens yield a pot of gold in the slots at the Lady Luck.

LEFT: Since it opened in 1956, Sam Boyd's Fremont Casino has been one of the landmark locations on Fremont Street, known more familiarly as Glitter Gulch.

The Early Days in the Nevada Desert

In the beginning, there was the land, an arid and forbidding land. The area that is now Nevada has always been a veritable wonderland of light and shadow, a world of stark but magnificent beauty.

The land itself speaks of something eternal and enduring. It is a message that is spoken through the color of the sunlight on shifting sands and the moonlight on the shadows of the rocks. It is spoken in the deceptive coolness of the desert morning as the landscape embraces the golden dawn. The mountains and canyons roll endlessly toward the horizon, forming an arid and cruel — yet beautiful — land.

Until the twentieth century, few people entered this forbidding environment. The Anasazi people — the "ancient ones" who built the great cities at Mesa Verde, Colorado and Canyon de Chelly, Arizona — passed through and built smaller settlements. But the Anasazi disappeared without a trace in the twelfth century and for 700 years most of present Nevada, and certainly the area around Las Vegas, was uninhabited except for a few Paiute and Shoshone nomads.

Nevada is a vast state with an area of 110,540 square miles consisting mostly of desert. It measures about 480 miles from north to south and about 320 miles from east to west, with the Colorado River forming a boundary on the southeast corner, separating the state of Nevada from the state of Arizona.

Nevada's name is a Spanish word, signifying "snow-clad," and was taken from the name of the western mountains, the Sierra Nevada, that separate the state from most of California. Until the 1950s, Nevada was known as the "Sagebrush State," because of the prevalence of several varieties of this plant, but it is more popularly called the "Silver State" because of the wealth of silver deposits, especially in the west central area near Reno.

Almost the entire area of Nevada exists within the vast tableland known as the Great Basin, a plateau with an average elevation of 4,500 feet that lies between the Wasatch Mountains on the east and the Sierra Nevada on the west. The surface of the basin is crossed by a series of parallel ridges,

ABOVE: In 1843, General John C. Fremont led his survey expedition into what is now Nevada, and crossed the rugged Sierra Nevada into California.

ABOVE: Great Basin desert, and the rugged Spring Mountains west of Las Vegas, are unchanged since before the first humans passed this way centuries ago.

OPPOSITE: This map shows Nevada as it existed in the 1890s. Las Vegas would be established on Las Vegas Wash in Vegas Valley at the southern tip. Clark County would be carved from Lincoln County.

some of which rise 9,000 feet above the plateau. These mountains are separated by canyons, valleys, and plains, most of which are deserts. In the summer, large areas are covered with plains of hard, sun-baked mud, as standing water in shallow lakes formed by run-off from melting snow gradually evaporates.

Most of the streams in Nevada are either absorbed by the sands of the desert or terminate in saline or alkaline lakes that have no outlet. In general, the state has dry, clear days and long periods of sunshine. Rains are typically heavy local downpours and thunderstorms are rare.

The earliest European visitors to the present state of Nevada were Franciscan friars who crossed

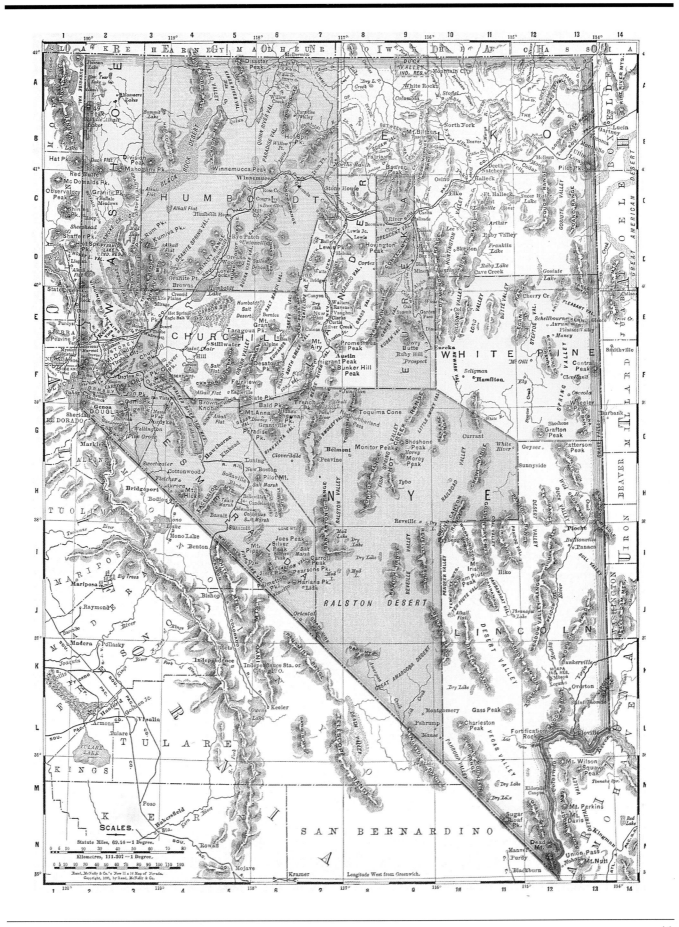

ABOVE: A pioneer wagon train reaches the Sierra Nevada. Most pioneers regarded Nevada simply as an obstacle.

OPPOSITE: Travelling through mountains of the West in the 1800s was no easy task.

the territory on their way to California in 1738. Other visitors were Peter Ogden, of Hudson's Bay Company, who discovered the Humboldt River in 1825 and the great mountain man and explorer Jedediah Smith, who crossed the region in 1826. General John C. Fremont led a survey expedition through what is now Nevada in 1843 and 1844, although at the time, the area was still part of Mexico. In 1848, the region that includes Nevada — as well as California, Utah and most of Arizona — became part of the United States under the terms of the Treaty of Guadalupe Hidalgo, which ended the Mexican War.

In 1849, during the great California Gold Rush, the first settlements in the part that is now

ABOVE: The Hotel Nevada, seen here as it appeared in 1906, was located at One Fremont Street. Today, the Golden Gate Hotel and Casino occupies this site.

Nevada were established on the Carson River by the Mormons. In 1850 the region extending westward from the Rocky Mountains to California (which is now Utah and Nevada) was organized as Utah Territory. The western part of the territory disagreed with the distant, Mormon-run government in Salt Lake City, however, and a separate government was soon established. After the refusal of its request for annexation to California, a petition was presented to Congress, and in 1861 the Territory of Nevada was established. On October 31, 1864, Nevada was admitted to the Union as the 36th state, but the area which includes present-day Las Vegas was not in what is now Nevada until 1866, when the land south of the 37th parallel was added

from Arizona. Its nickname at the time was "Battle Born State," because it was admitted during the Civil War in a ploy to keep its mineral wealth out of the hands of the Confederacy.

Until 1859, the population of Nevada numbered only 1,000, and consisted mainly of Mormons and California gold seekers who had stopped on the way west. Following the discovery of silver in the Comstock Lode near Carson City, there was a massive influx of miners, and within two years several important towns sprang up.

The Comstock Lode became the richest silver-mining center in the world, and remained so for over a quarter century. With the decline of the output of the Comstock mines, and the demoneti-

ABOVE: When Las Vegas bloomed in the 1940s, Fremont Street remained its hub. The Boulder Club and the Hotel Apache were already venerable landmarks. Benny Binion's Horseshoe Club was originally the Eldorado.

ABOVE: Gaming was one of the diversions available to the hard-working miners who toiled in the gold fields and the silver mines of Nevada's Comstock Lode.

OPPOSITE: The Comstock, like California's Mother Lode, offered a chance for great wealth, but first you had to get there.

zation of silver in the last quarter of the nineteenth century, the state fell into decline, and lost one-third of its people. The 1890 population numbered a mere 45,761. With the opening years of the twentieth century, however, a revival set in when gold mines were discovered southeast of the Comstock region, and the application of the cyanide process to the older mines put new life into the state's mining interests. The development of sheep raising, the construction of irrigation projects and the building of transcontinental railroad lines also contributed to this revival.

The place that is now Las Vegas was once a camp site used from the late 1820s by people travelling west to California on the Old Spanish Trail.

ABOVE: Only a handful of the travellers who crossed Nevada on their way to California stopped longer than it took to rest their livestock overnight.

The fact that the word "Vegas" means "meadows" tells us that the Mexicans knew that horses could graze there, and that they had discovered the artesian springs that provided water for them and their livestock. Since the land which is now Nevada was part of Utah Territory in the years after it was "ceded" by Mexico, it was within the sphere of influence of the Mormon Church. With this in mind, it is not surprising that the first permanent, non-Indian settlement at Las Vegas would have been a Mormon settlement. In 1855, Mormon leader Brigham Young sent missionary William

Bringhurst with a team of 30 into the area from Salt Lake City to set up a mission where Indians could be taught agriculture and be converted to the Mormon faith.

The settlement endured for only two years, and it was gradually supplanted by a trading post that serviced miners working in the surrounding area. A German gold miner named Octavius Gass arrived in a mini-gold rush that occurred in the 1860s, just before statehood. By 1865, this "Dutchman" (as all Germans in the Old West seemed to be called) had moved into the old

ABOVE: Downtown Las Vegas as it appeared when the city was founded in 1905. The Arizona Club would remain a popular place of recreation for many years.

ABOVE: One could always find a game going at one of the tables in the Wellington Saloon, which was located on the road south of Las Vegas.

adobes built by Bringhurst's Mormon group and established a ranch that he called El Rancho Las Vegas. The Gass ranch was the first real precursor to the present city of Las Vegas. In addition to his cattle and his orchards, Gass made wine and raised other food, which he sold to travellers. Also offered, as in most similar Western outposts, were card playing and other games of chance which the tourists could enjoy during their stopover.

A major boom for the area came at the turn of the century, when William Clark bought the 640-acre El Rancho Las Vegas. Clark was a senator from Montana, who had connections to the Union Pacific Railroad. He had also built the San Pedro, Los Angeles & Salt Lake Railroad. In 1905, the Union Pacific decided to establish a major east-west route through the area because, they said, of the availability of water.

ABOVE: This early view of downtown Las Vegas probably dates from about 1910 when electricity first came to what was later to be America's city of lights.

It was in 1905 that the town of Las Vegas was established. Land was auctioned off and soon the population grew from less than 100 to nearly 1,500. By 1911, when the town was officially incorporated, a tent camp had started giving way to clapboard buildings, and electric street lights had been installed on Fremont Street, the main boulevard leading east into town from the Union Pacific station. Though gaming had been officially banned by the state of Nevada in 1909, visitors to Las Vegas could still find a game.

In 1905, the land auction that started the Las Vegas townsite was held at the Union Pacific Railroad, on a dirt intersection off Fremont and Main streets. The first three lots on the corner, at One Fremont Street, sold for a total of $1,750. When the first hotel opened here in 1906, it was

called the "Hotel Nevada." The name would be changed in 1931 to the "Sal Sagev," or Las Vegas spelled backwards. It was finally to be re-named as the "Golden Gate." As the first hotel in southern Nevada to be built of concrete, it was able to endure the test of time and survive amidst the constant changes on Fremont Street. The first telephone in Las Vegas was installed at the hotel in 1907. The phone number was "1."

Named for the senator, Clark County was created in February 1908, having been carved from what was formerly Lincoln County. With Las Vegas as its county seat, Clark covers 7,881 square miles, which is comparable to the area of Massachusetts.

This set the stage for the development of what would one day become Nevada's largest city, and perhaps the most exciting city in the world.

Coming of Age in the Nevada Desert

With Hoover Dam providing the energy to keep the electric lights flashing all night, Las Vegas became a glamourous place to be. The sleepy cowboy town was on the way to becoming the playground where Hollywood's stars came to relax, party and do a bit of gaming.

Just as the arrival of the Union Pacific had guaranteed the survival of Las Vegas as a town, another great engineering project would guarantee the city's success. By the 1920s, the goal of bringing electric power to every corner of the United States had become a national priority. In the East, great coal-fired plants were already in service, but in the West, with its high mountains and surging rivers, hydro-electric power was an alternative. On the part of the Colorado River forming the border between Nevada and Arizona, at a place only 30 miles south of Las Vegas, there was a narrow canyon known as Boulder Canyon. It was determined to be a perfect place for the construction of a hydro-electric dam, and Congress authorized construction of such an edifice in 1928.

When it was completed in 1936, Boulder Dam was hailed as "the eighth wonder of the world." At 726 feet, it was the highest dam ever constructed by human hands. It took 4.4 million cubic yards of concrete and backed up over 30 million acre feet of water. More important for Las Vegas, however, was the fact that the dam had brought thousands of workers to spend their pay checks in the city, and when they were gone, the dam brought tourists and provided virtually limitless electricity to power the lights that were appearing on the marquees of Fremont Street.

The dam itself was originally called Hoover Dam, but that name was changed in 1930 while the dam was still under construction because former President Herbert Hoover had fallen into disfavor for his supposed failure to deal with the Great Depression. It remained as Boulder Dam until 1947, when the original, and present, name was restored.

Meanwhile, in 1931, the legislature of Nevada had taken the historic step of making wagering legal in the state for the first time since 1909. The first Nevada gaming license was issued to the Northern Club on Fremont Street. Two years later, the United States Congress repealed

ABOVE: When it was completed in 1936, Boulder Dam (later Hoover Dam) was the largest in the world. It is still a major sightseeing diversion for Las Vegas visitors.

ABOVE AND RIGHT: These 1933-1934 photographs by B.D. Glaha show the monumental scale of the Boulder Dam project, as well as a few of the thousands of workers who'd spend their pay under the marquees of Fremont Street.

ABOVE: Spinning a roulette wheel at a Las Vegas casino, during the annual "Helldorado" celebration, circa 1930s.

OPPOSITE: Mr. and Mrs. E.W. Cragin celebrate with a few of their friends in the bar at the Hotel Apache.

Prohibition, and beverages could now be enjoyed by patrons of the gaming establishments. These steps, combined with the huge population of workers on the dam project, made Las Vegas a robust and lively town. The first major hotel, the 100-room Apache, had opened in 1932 and the downtown area around Fremont Street became the epicenter of action.

The Fremont Street downtown district would remain as the tourist mecca for another two decades, although developments were beginning to spring up elsewhere, specifically on Las Vegas Boulevard, which crossed Fremont Street five

ABOVE: Even in the 1940s, Las Vegas had establishments that served their customers 24 hours a day.

OPPOSITE: Las Vegas native Alta Ham, dressed in her cowgirl attire, enjoys a laugh with friends and others. To her right is an unidentified cowboy actor who was in town for the filming of the 1929 feature film *Water*, one of the first of many motion pictures made in and around Las Vegas.

blocks east of the Union Pacific station. Though it was not yet known as "the Strip," Las Vegas Boulevard was already the major north-south route through town, with both US Highway 93 and US Highway 95 sharing it.

The first major hotel complex on Las Vegas Boulevard was El Rancho Las Vegas, named for the original settlement and located about three miles south of Fremont Street. It opened in 1941, and was followed a year later by the Last Frontier Hotel, which later became the New Frontier, and in turn evolved into the present-day Frontier.

The Last Frontier was one of the first hotels to bring a big-name Hollywood celebrity into town to entertain in its showroom. Sophie Tucker did a two-week stand and thus started a trend that would continue for decades. Las Vegas was on the way to becoming a playground for Hollywood's top glitterati. All of Hollywood's stars travelled up to Las Vegas to relax, party and do a bit of gaming.

Meanwhile, Reno was also evolving as an important tourist and gaming center. Indeed, until as late as the 1950s, Reno would remain as the state's metropolis. In the 1940 census, Reno had a population of 21,317 to only 8,422 for Las Vegas. However, by 1950, Reno had grown to 32,497, but Las Vegas had mushroomed to 24,624.

RIGHT: The Las Vegas Post Office was designed in the same Spanish colonial-style architecture as other public buildings and and quasi-public buildings. The latter included the nearby Union Pacific station at the head of Fremont Street. As with most small Western towns, Las Vegas came into being because of the arrival of the railroad and depended on it as a lifeline, bringing supplies and tourists. By the 1940s, however, US Highways 91, 93 and 95 had taken away the railroad's monopoly.

RIGHT: Fremont Street in 1943 was a bustling, vibrant city center. As is evident from the highway signs, both US Highways 91 and 93 used Fremont Street. The Union Pacific logo can be seen on the train station at the head of the street, but Western Air Lines already had a ticket desk at the Hotel Apache.

RIGHT: This nighttime, Christmas season view of Fremont Street looks west as does the view on the previous pages. This photo was taken in the late 1940s after the Pioneer Club had erected its first neon cowboy.

The Golden Age of Las Vegas

It was the beginning of an era in which Las Vegas would be transformed. The wall of hotel/casinos dotting Las Vegas Boulevard had earned the area a new and enduring nickname.
If Fremont Street was "Glitter Gulch," Las Vegas Boulevard was simply "the Strip."

By the late 1940s, Fremont Street was being referred to as "Glitter Gulch," a place of bright lights and non-stop entertainment that never closed. The Golden Nugget and the Eldorado opened in 1946, with the Golden Nugget being the first structure designed from the ground up to be a casino. In 1951, when Binion's Horseshoe Club (formerly the Eldorado) started hosting the World Series of Poker, it ensured its lasting place as one of the most important Glitter Gulch venues, and it made ex-cowboy Benny Binion a very wealthy man.

While Fremont Street cultivated a Las Vegas image that focussed on the city's roots in the "Old West," with neon cowboys and cowgirls, the properties that would soon proliferate on Las Vegas Boulevard began to develop a mood that mirrored that of Hollywood. It was in 1946, the same year that the Nugget and Eldorado opened downtown, that Benjamin "Bugsy" Siegel, along with Charles "Lucky" Luciano and other alleged underworld characters, opened the Flamingo Hotel on Las Vegas Boulevard, about a mile south of El Rancho Las Vegas, near what was essentially the edge of town on the highway leading to Los Angeles. If one was driving in from Hollywood, the Flamingo was the first major landmark. It was also one of the first to offer Hollywood-style entertainment. Jimmy Durante opened the Flamingo showroom, which was soon featuring those perennial Las Vegas stage favorites, Dean Martin and Jerry Lewis. Meanwhile, another long-time Las Vegas show-stage fixture, Sammy Davis, Jr., opened across Las Vegas Boulevard at the Frontier (which was then the Last Frontier).

It was the beginning of an era in which Las Vegas would be transformed from a little western town into a "Second Hollywood," and a city that rivaled the original for its non-stop party atmosphere. Soon there was such a wall of hotel/casinos dotting Las Vegas Boulevard that it had earned a new and enduring nickname. If Fremont Street was

ABOVE: When it opened in 1955, the nine-story Riviera Hotel and Casino was considered *the* skyscraper of Las Vegas.

RIGHT: Opened in 1941, El Rancho Las Vegas was the first hotel on the Strip. At that time, Las Vegas Boulevard South was still the edge of town. As the story goes, California hotel operator Thomas Hull was driving into town when his car broke down on this spot. While waiting for help, he started counting cars and decided that this would be the place to build a new property. He built El Rancho, invited a host of Hollywood stars to his grand opening, and the Golden Age of Las Vegas began.

ABOVE: Glitter Gulch by night, circa 1946, the year that both the Golden Nugget and the Eldorado opened at Second and Fremont.

"Glitter Gulch," Las Vegas Boulevard was simply "the Strip."

In 1959, another interesting Las Vegas tradition was born as the Golden Gate Hotel and Casino on Fremont Street introduced shrimp cocktails to the casino scene. The price was 50 cents, and this would not change for 32 years. Shrimp cocktail soon became a favorite among casino clientele, and many other casinos began promoting their version of this Golden Gate special. However, the Golden Gate has won every *Review Journal* "Best of Las Vegas" contest for shrimp cocktail and it has become a Las Vegas institution. Although the Golden Gate is a small property, it has served nearly two tons of high-quality shrimp

every week since 1959. A generous portion is served to each customer in an old-fashioned "tulip" sundae glass. The recipe is, of course, a secret.

On September 26, 1991, the Golden Gate Hotel and Casino would celebrate the sale of the 25 millionth helping of its signature shrimp cocktail. In true Las Vegas fashion, the event was marked by the attendance of the four Las Vegas mayors whose collective terms in office spanned the years since the first Golden Gate shrimp cocktail was served in 1959. Then-current Mayor Jan Jones was joined by former Mayors Oran Gragson, Dill Braire and Ron Lurie. The world's largest shrimp cocktail was created for the celebration,

ABOVE: It was in 1947 that Benny Binion came to town, bought the Eldorado and changed the name to the Horseshoe. The Horseshoe still has the highest betting limit in town.

RIGHT: The 1952 film *Las Vegas Story* captured the growing mood of sophistication in the city. It featured Jane Russell as a singer sought by former boyfriend Victor Mature. Vincent Price played Jane's husband and Hoagy Carmichael held forth with the band.

with a monolithic reproduction of the Golden Gate's cocktail glass was carved from a solid block of ice weighing over 1,200 pounds, then filled with over 200 pounds of shrimp and topped with gallons of cocktail sauce.

The Golden Nugget was the first Las Vegas property to be opened specifically as a hotel-casino, but by the 1950s, every major property to be built in town was just that — with the addition of a major showroom to help draw patrons. The nine-story Riviera was the "skyscraper" of Las Vegas properties when it opened on the Strip in 1955. Another Las Vegas landmark, which was the opening act at the Riviera: Wladziu Liberace — traditionally known only by his surname — was a flamboyant yet gifted pianist, whose glittering costumes would come to overshadow his considerable musical talent, but which became a fixture in Las Vegas iconography.

On April 20, 1955, Liberace cut the ribbon to open the Riviera. The reigning king of entertainment, a wavy-haired pianist with a flair for fur capes and rhinestone jewelry, Liberace arrived with his 23-piece orchestra. He opened the $10 million Riviera as the first headliner, with actress Joan Crawford serving as official hostess. The grand opening attracted worldwide attention — every guest room in the city was sold out. An avant garde fashion designer named Christian Dior created Liberace's dazzling white tuxedo, and the Riviera's Clover Room theater was draped with platinum gray velour under a jet black ceiling illuminated by "starlight" constellations.

The extravaganza drew reviews from Hollywood columnists — and raised eyebrows from their readers. By paying Liberace an astounding $50,000 per week (an unheard-of sum considering homes could be bought for less than $10,000) the Riviera had made entertainment history. The resort also gained distinction as the

ABOVE: Nine fingers for nine stories. When the Riviera was designed, a building of this size was revolutionary for Las Vegas. It helped make the Strip the place to be.

town's first high-rise hotel with a nine-story tower, 300 deluxe rooms and a neo-modern, rock-and-masonry facade that sharply deviated from the frontier-style architecture prevalent in Las Vegas at the time. Inside, the new resort was lavishly decorated with wormwood paneling, fleur-de-lis wallpaper and brass and walnut sculpture.

The entire ninth floor contained luxury penthouse suites with satin drapes and upholstery, as well as individual cocktail bars. In addition to the Clover Room supper club, the Riviera featured the Hickory Room restaurant, Cafe Noir coffee shop, one main bar and three service bars, an Olympic-sized swimming pool and landscaping

ABOVE: Lively roulette action at one of the Strip casinos. The lady at the head of the table certainly exudes a sense of confidence. The lady at the right is also having a good time.

RIGHT: This view looking east on Fremont Street from the Union Pacific station certainly shows how Fremont Street came to be known as Glitter Gulch.

ABOVE: Coraleen Jurian crowns Liberace with a cowboy hat, circa 1955. Liberace's glamorous shows at the Riviera helped add a dimension of style to the erstwhile cowboy town.

enhanced by garden paths, flower beds and redwood trees imported from California. The fast-paced casino contained 18 table games and 116 slot machines and, though modest by today's standards, it was considered the place for high-rollers.

Over the ensuing decade, the Riviera continued its leading role as an entertainment center for Las Vegas. Among the stars who graced the Clover Room's stage during the 1950s were Hollywood luminaries such as Harry Belafonte, Milton Berle, Orson Welles, Dinah Shore, Zsa Zsa Gabor, Ginger Rogers, Mickey Rooney, Red Skelton and Marlene Dietrich.

In 1960, the Riviera renamed the Clover Room as the Versailles Theatre, and headliner celebrities such as Carol Channing, Louis Armstrong, Tony Martin, Cyd Charisse, George Burns, Eddie Fisher, Tony Bennett, Dean Martin and Sarah Vaughan were frequent performers. During the 1960s, up-and-coming performers such as Juliet Prowse, Engelbert Humperdink, Connie Francis, Johnny Mathis, Barbra Streisand and Ann-Margaret, were all featured on the Versailles stage. The Riviera added four championship tennis courts near the pool in 1972, and they were later to be the site of the Dewar's Celebrity-Pro Tennis Tournament, which drew top professional athletes from around the world.

Three years later, the hotel completed its 17-story Monte Carlo tower at a cost of $20 million. It consisted of 300 rooms, 60 suites, and an elaborate penthouse, giving the Riviera a total of 1,000 guest rooms. In 1977, the $6 million San Remo tower added 200 rooms to the south side of the resort, as well as the Ristorante Italiano, a 100-seat gourmet Italian restaurant.

Throughout the 1950s, a building boom had made the Strip the place to be in Las Vegas. The Flamingo and Riviera were soon joined by the Dunes, the Sands and the Tropicana, and the Last

Frontier became the New Frontier. The Showboat opened on the opposite end of Fremont Street, east of the Strip, offering bowling alleys and buffet meals.

The idea of "theme" properties that would be so popular in the 1990s had an early precursor in the 1960s. This was the Circus Circus Hotel Casino which opened on the Strip in October, 1968 as the only gaming establishment in the world offering entertainment for all ages. Initially, Circus Circus was just a combination of casino, carnival midway and the world's largest permanent circus tent. The 400-room hotel was added in 1972. The casino occupies the main floor of the building, while the

ABOVE: Liberace and Elvis during a lighter moment at the Riviera in November 1957. For this photo shoot, the two stars swapped jackets and musical instruments.

THE ILLUSTRATED HISTORY OF LAS VEGAS

RIGHT: Looking west on Fremont Street from near Second Street. In 1946, there were already plenty of taxi cabs working Glitter Gulch. Perhaps one of them carries Benny Binion, who had just come to town to close the deal to make the Eldorado his own.

second floor is filled with live carnival games, state-of-the-art arcade games and free circus arena in which trapeze fliers, high-wire daredevils, acrobats, jugglers, aerialists and clowns entertain. Within the resort complex there are about 2,800 rooms, a variety of dining areas that cater to all appetites and budgets, a shopping promenade, a 10,000-square-foot race and sports book and more. Circus Circus is also home to Grand Slam Canyon, a five-acre, climate-controlled, indoor amusement park.

As early as the 1950s, an unprecedented increase in the amount of money spilling across the tables in Las Vegas led to allegations of underworld connections and possible illegal activities, so the state of Nevada moved to strengthen gaming control. The Gaming Control Board was created within the Nevada Tax Commission by the state legislature in 1955, and four years later, it evolved into the Nevada Gaming Commission.

Within the next two decades, the Nevada legislature would take several other important steps to encourage the profitability of the gaming industry. It was in 1967 that it became legal for publicly traded corporations to have gaming licenses. This would pave the way for major hotel chains to get into the act in Las Vegas. In 1977 — the same year that gaming revenues in Clark County exceeded a billion dollars annually — the legislature made it possible for Nevada-based casino owners to operate out of state casinos, and soon many of the best-known names on the Las Vegas scene opened properties in Atlantic City, New Jersey.

Factors other than gaming and showroom entertainment also helped to increase the flow of visitors to Las Vegas in the 1950s and 1960s. Liberal marriage and divorce laws — including a marriage license bureau that is open 24 hours a day on weekends — brought patrons for both, as dozens of wedding chapels proliferated on Las Vegas Boulevard and elsewhere in town. The

ABOVE: The coffee shop at the Showboat catered to the regular folks and tourists who were just passing through, or in town for the weekend.

1840-26

Desert Inn opened an 18-hole golf course, and began hosting the PGA Tournament of Champions.

Nevertheless, the penultimate Las Vegas sport — after gaming, of course — in the 1950s and 1960s was celebrity watching. And no celebrities epitomized the era better than the five entertainers known collectively as "the Rat Pack" because they were often seen together and were usually seen at one anothers' parties. The three weeks in January

ABOVE: George Tobias carefully observes a card game in the 1956 film *The Tattered Dress*. Also in the cast were Jeff Chandler, Jeanne Crain, Elaine Stewart and Jack Carson.

RIGHT: When it was completed on Fremont Street in 1956, the 15-story Fremont Hotel was the tallest building in Las Vegas. Down on the street, Glitter Gulch was booming.

1960 when they all appeared in a "summit conference" at the Sands is still marked as a milestone in Las Vegas history. Most well known of the "Pack" was "Chairman of the Board" Frank Sinatra, one of the century's most enduringly popular singers who was then at the peak of his popularity as both a singer and actor. The other members included Dean Martin and Sammy Davis, Jr., who were also actor/singers at the peak of their careers and already familiar to Las Vegas show-goers, as well as B-movie comedian Joey Bishop and actor Peter Lawford, who is best remembered for his 12-year marriage to Pat Kennedy, sister of President John F. Kennedy. After the "historic" summit conference in 1960, the members of the Rat Pack, especially Dean Martin and Sammy Davis, Jr., continued to be important fixtures on the Las Vegas scene for over two decades.

Not all the Las Vegas celebrities of the era were entertainers, and not all were visible on stage or at the see-and-be-seen parties that were so common. In 1966, the reclusive billionaire Howard Hughes began buying property in Las Vegas, including the Desert Inn. Between 1966 and 1970, Hughes took up residence on the top floor of the Desert Inn, shutting himself off from the world and managing his far-flung business empire through shadowy layers of intermediaries.

He became somewhat of a legend in Las Vegas folklore because his obsessive-compulsive disorder and germ phobia made it impossible for him to leave his lavish suite and face other human beings other than a small circle of bodyguards. He was never seen in public, but people driving past the Desert Inn on Las Vegas Boulevard knew he was in there, and for four years, Hughes was Las Vegas's favorite mystery man. Hughes later moved out of the United States. He spent most of the years leading up to his death in 1976 living in Latin America and the Caribbean.

Las Vegas was progressively becoming a more glamorous place, with more and more lavish prop-

ABOVE: When the Showboat opened in 1954, overlooking the pool was (what else?) a showboat!

erties springing up along the Strip. One of the first great theme properties, the Roman-Empire-themed Caesars Palace, opened on August 5, 1966 at the heart of the Strip, constructed in a majestic Greco-Roman style at a cost of $25 million in 1960s dollars. Graced by fountains and gleaming marble reproductions of classic statuary, the hotel has two pools, one of which is Olympic sized, inlaid with imported marble and designed in the shape of a Roman shield. At the entrance to the central people mover was a rotunda that housed a miniature city of Rome as it may have looked 2,000 years ago. At the north property border was the now-legendary Quadriga statue — four golden horses and a charioteer who beckoned visitors into the casino.

With Caesars Palace, and bustling showrooms everywhere, Las Vegas had clearly attained its status as an exciting and very glamorous place.

ABOVE: In the 1955 film *Las Vegas Shakedown*, Dennis O'Keefe played an honest casino operator who played it straight with his patrons. The film also starred Charles Winninger and Coleen Gray.

LEFT: The Liberace Museum on Tropicana Avenue is a lasting tribute to one of Las Vegas' greatest showmen.

INSET, ABOVE: In this rare 1955 photo, Liberace is seen embracing Mrs. Elmer Robinson at a party given by Marshall Wright of the Riviera. Liberace's mother is seen in the background.

At the museum, the great entertainer's stunning collection of costumes and memorabilia is on display to the public to benefit his charitable foundation. Included are his legendary candelabras, his $60,000 chinchilla cape, various diamond-studded costumes, a mirror-covered Rolls-Royce and the world's largest rhinestone, weighing over 50 pounds.

RIGHT: The Four Queens opened in 1966 across Fremont Street from the Fremont Hotel. It completed the atmosphere for what would be Glitter Gulch's most glittering intersection. The "four queens" were actually the owner's four daughters.

RIGHT: The 1959 Warner Brothers film *Oceans Eleven* featured a stage full of legendary Las Vegas showgirls and plenty of action, but it is most famous for being the film that starred the entire Rat Pack. Peter Lawford; Sammy Davis, Jr.; Frank Sinatra; Dean Martin and Joey Bishop played army buddies set on robbing five Las Vegas casinos.

RIGHT: This excellent aerial view of the Strip from the 1950s shows the hotel tower at the Sands as well as the sprawling Sands complex. Also of interest are the large number of open lots that still existed along the Strip. Treasure Island and the Mirage now occupy the area at the lower left.

ABOVE, TOP: The Rat Pack on stage at the Sands during the 1960 "Summit Conference." From left, Peter Lawford; Sammy Davis, Jr.; Frank Sinatra; Dean Martin and Joey Bishop.

ABOVE: Rat Packers Dean Martin and Frank Sinatra cut up on the Sands stage.

RIGHT: Sammy Davis, Jr. holds his own on a Las Vegas stage in the 1967 Screen Gems film, *Pepe.*

LEFT: Rat Pack members Frank Sinatra and Sammy Davis, Jr. are introduced by Dean Martin on stage at the Sands in January 1960. The summit conference was the hottest ticket Las Vegas had ever seen.

From the Elvis Years to the 1980s

Elvis Presley dominated the Las Vegas show scene in his brilliant white jumpsuit from 1969 through the mid-1970s. Though he is gone, he continues to symbolize the glamour and the vital energy that was, and would always be, Las Vegas. Though others will come and go, Elvis will always be the king.

The Rat Pack epitomized the Las Vegas of the 1950s and 1960s, but no entertainer epitomized the Las Vegas of the 1970s better than Elvis Presley. A major figure in the birth of rock and roll in the 1950s, Elvis had become a successful, if not critically-acclaimed, B-movie star in the 1960s. He had also spent some time in Las Vegas during the 1960s. In 1964, he came to town to film one of his most memorable movies, the appropriately-titled *Viva Las Vegas*. In this film, directed for Metro-Goldwyn-Mayer by George Sidney, Elvis portrayed "Lucky," an aspiring race-car driver in pursuit of a hot-blooded young swimming instructor, played by another familiar Las Vegas performer, Ann-Margaret.

On May 1, 1967, Elvis made one of his most memorable appearances in Las Vegas when he flew in aboard Frank Sinatra's private jet to marry his long-time live-in girlfriend, Priscilla Beaulieu. The famous wedding was to be a civil ceremony at the brand-new Aladdin Hotel on the Strip.

Despite being an occasional celebrity-about-town, Elvis had not appeared on stage in Las Vegas since a brief stand at the New Frontier in 1956. As the 1960s came to an end, Elvis was eager to get back on stage as a rock performer, and his manager, Andreas van Kuijk (aka Colonel Tom Parker), decided that Las Vegas would be the ideal venue for the comeback of the once and future "King of Rock and Roll."

When Elvis Presley's successful "Comeback Special" aired on television in December 1968, it paved the way for the "Colonel" to negotiate a near-million dollar deal with the newly-completed International Hotel (now the Las Vegas Hilton) on Paradise Road, a block east of the Strip. The King opened his 28-day stand at the International on July 29, 1969. Elvis was instantly the hottest show in town and the most important show to come to Las Vegas since the Rat Pack's summit conference a decade earlier. When Elvis returned to the International in January 1971, his anxiously-await-

ABOVE: There have been many great headliners in Las Vegas through the years, but Elvis Presley created an ethos that has never been equalled or surpassed.

1812-45

ABOVE: In this scene from *Viva Las Vegas*, a racing driver named Lucky (Elvis Presley) and an international playboy named Count Mancini (Cesare Danova) search Las Vegas stages for a beautiful woman (played by Ann-Margret) they'd met only once.

OPPOSITE: In another scene from *Viva Las Vegas*, Lucky (Elvis Presley) has at last found his love interest (Ann-Margret).

ed stand was an even hotter ticket than it had been in the summer of 1969. Elvis made Las Vegas a routine part of his tour schedule. By the time he came back again in January 1972, the International was the Las Vegas Hilton, but Elvis was still the King. He continued to return to Las Vegas through the middle years of the 1970s. He strode on stage in his brilliant white jumpsuit to the strains of *Also Sprach Zarathustra*, launched into *See See Rider*, and became one of Las Vegas's most lasting legends. Indeed, he came to symbolize the glamour and the vital energy that was, and would continue to be, Las Vegas.

After Elvis' sad and untimely death in 1977, there was no-one that could take his place.

ABOVE: Ann-Margret on the stage at the Las Vegas Hilton. She was one of the most important Las Vegas showroom stars of the 1970s.

RIGHT: A bevy of beautiful young women surround a gaming table in a scene from the 1969 United Artists film *Where It's At.* The film starred Rosemary Forsyth and Brenda Vaccaro, as well as Don Rickles, and it was filmed on location at Caesars Palace.

ABOVE: Elvis Presley reviews construction of his stage at the International Hotel (later Las Vegas Hilton).

OPPOSITE: Liza Minnelli welcomes Sammy Davis, Jr. onto the stage at the Las Vegas Hilton. They were two of the most memorable stars to grace the Las Vegas stage.

However, to this day, his memory lives through the Elvis impersonators that pay tribute to his great Las Vegas shows. The 1992 film, *Honeymoon In Vegas*, in turn, paid tribute to the Elvis impersonators through its climactic scene which involved a plane-load of skydivers in jumpsuits called the "Flying Elvises" who parachuted onto the strip at night.

Today, an "Elvis" show — particularly the "Legends" concert at the Imperial Palace — can be seen almost every night in Las Vegas.

The 1970s also saw a new generation of entertainers come into town as successors to the people of the Rat Pack era. Elvis *Viva Las Vegas* co-star Ann-Margaret appeared, as did other popular

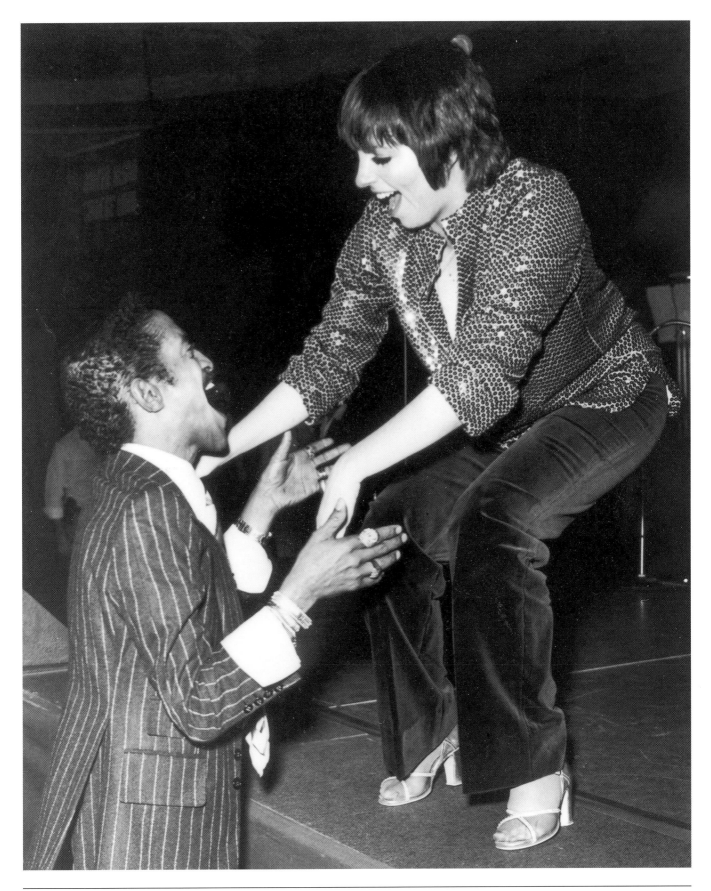

ABOVE: Two views showing the evolution of the Lady Luck Casino. The bottom photo is the original building, which opened in 1964.

OPPOSITE: Gaming fun at the Dunes Casino in the early 1970s. Opened in 1955, the Dunes was closed in 1993.

singers such as Neil Diamond, Tina Turner and Jose Feliciano, and comedians from Steve Martin to Bill Cosby. People with popular television variety shows — from Johnny Carson to Johnny Cash to Sonny and Cher — also brought their live shows to Las Vegas.

During the 1970s, the Riviera, which had opened its showroom in the 1950s with Liberace, now featured the Fifth Dimension, the Carpenters, Don Rickles, Dionne Warwick, the Righteous Brothers, Olivia Newton-John, Barry Manilow and Gladys Knight and the Pips.

As the 1980s began with the Golden Anniversary of Gaming in 1981, the showroom focus turned from the glitz of Hollywood entertainers to Las Vegas roots and country music. Dolly Parton and Kenny Rogers both headlined, as did country "outlaws" such as Willie Nelson, Kris Kristofferson and Hank Williams, Jr. Comedians

ABOVE: Enjoying the action at Caesars Palace, as seen in the 1969 film, *Where It's At.*

ABOVE, TOP: The Showboat, as it appeared in 1970.

OPPOSITE: When it was erected in 1990, the Showboat's marquee was the world's largest electric sign.

that took the stage in Las Vegas during the 1980s included such perennial favorites as Don Rickles and Rich Little, as well as newcomers such as Rodney Dangerfield and Roseanne. The Las Vegas era of mega-headliners also continued into the 1980s, with the Riviera featuring stars such as Shirley MacLaine, Liza Minnelli, Bob Newhart, Glen Campbell, Joan Rivers, Bill Cosby and the "chairman of the board," Frank Sinatra.

Change, however, was on the horizon. The escalating price war for showroom headliners reached a peak in the early 1980s, with many celebrities unable to generate audiences to justify their huge salaries. Recognizing the evolving taste of the American public, many properties on the Strip and around town began to change their formats.

In 1985, the Riviera took a bold step toward providing a new style of showroom entertainment, one that they felt would appeal to a broader base of Las Vegas audiences. On June 21, the Riviera unveiled Jeff Kutash's "Splash," an all-new production that captivated audiences and garnered an unprecedented number of awards for best production show in Las Vegas. The "aquacade of music

and dance" took place in and around a 20,000-gallon aquarium while featuring numerous performers and specialty acts. Later that year the Riviera introduced Norbert Aleman's "An Evening at La Cage," a Parisian style revue of female impersonators and cabaret dancers. Over the next two years the resort installed a basement-style comedy club called the Improv, and a fantasie de Paris that is called "Crazy Girls: Las Vegas' Sexiest Topless Revue." This presentation of four production shows, which still continues, has never been duplicated by another Las Vegas resort. Moreover, the popularity of the productions continues to grow, even as audience levels approach the 10 million mark.

A new 24-story Monaco Tower costing $28 million opened in 1988, nearly doubling the size of the Riviera to 2,100 rooms. Two years later the Riviera expanded its casino by 70,000 square feet to a total of nearly 125,000 square feet, making it one of the largest casinos in the world.

Meanwhile, the Las Vegas population was growing by leaps and bounds, from 64,405 in 1960 to 164,674 in 1980 and 258,295 in 1990 to 363,171 in 1995, with Clark County having 1,016,177 people.

The Clark County Department of Comprehensive Planning estimated that between 4,000 and 6,000 people were moving into the county monthly, making Las Vegas the fastest growing city in the United States. More than 28 million people visit Las Vegas annually. Most visitors come for the gaming, and are served by establishments holding 1,200 gaming licenses and equipped with over 122,800 slot machines and nearly 4,000 table games.

ABOVE: Louis Armstrong, with Pearl Bailey, on stage at the Las Vegas Hilton.

OPPOSITE: Wayne Newton joins Bob Hope at the Las Vegas Hilton. In the 1980s, Newton was one of the city's top stars.

Many visitors also come to Las Vegas for conventions held at the Las Vegas Convention Center and elsewhere. Over 2,700 conventions are held in Clark County annually, attended by more than 2.6 million delegates. The Las Vegas Convention Center alone totals 1.6 million total square feet, including ten exhibit halls and 89 meeting rooms with a total of 149,862 square

ABOVE: The world-famous Chapel of the Bells is conveniently located on the Strip at the Fun City Motel.

OPPOSITE: A Little White Chapel offers a drive-up window, but we don't know whether Joan Collins made use of this feature.

feet. In addition, private convention space boosts the total to 3.3 million square feet. Meanwhile, the Cashman Field Center consists of two exhibit halls and 16 meeting rooms covering 17,500 square feet, with a 10,000-seat stadium and a 2,000-seat theater. Las Vegas McCarran International Airport, less than a mile from the Strip and three miles from the Convention Center, is ranked as the eighth busiest in the world.

Las Vegas is also a popular destination for weddings, with over 35 wedding chapels and nearly 100,000 marriage licenses issued annually, including nearly 2,500 on Valentine's Day alone.

BELOW: The East Tower is a new addition to the very popular Lady Luck Casino Hotel, located on North Third Street.

RIGHT: Two important classic properties located mid-Strip are the Frontier, which opened in 1943 as the Last Frontier, and the Desert Inn, which opened in 1950. The Desert Inn is famous as having been the home of Howard Hughes, when the eccentric billionaire was in residence in Las Vegas.

The Theme Hotels of the 1990s

Las Vegas had become the ultimate fantasy land. One could travel back in time to the Caribbean of the eighteenth century, to Medieval Britain, or to the Roman Empire. One could stroll from the old West to a tropical rain forest or a three-ring circus.

The 1990s saw the beginning of a new era in Las Vegas, a hotel/casino building boom that would be characterized by a series of incredible "theme" resorts. When it was completed in November 1989, the Mirage was the first new resort built in the city in 15 years. This destination resort, with its South Seas tropical theme, has become the most successful property in the history of the gaming and hospitality industries. It ignited a $5 billion expansion in Las Vegas which catapulted the city into the having its distinction as the fastest growing city in America and the number one tourism destination in the country.

"The Mirage will usher in a new Las Vegas," promised Stephen A. "Steve" Wynn, chairman of the board of Mirage Resorts, Incorporated, prior to the resort's opening. "Our goal was to build a hotel so overriding in its stature, that it would be a reason in and of itself for visitors to come to Las Vegas in much the same way that Disney attracts people to Orlando, Florida. We knew others would try to

mirror the success of the Mirage, perhaps [thinking] that we would even build another property, which we have, but we never anticipated the intensity and speed with which these properties would proliferate."

The "new" Las Vegas, featuring Treasure Island's mock sea battle, the Luxor pyramid and the MGM Grand — the world's largest hotel — began to attract a vacationing public that largely bypassed the city in the past. In 1995, a record 29 million people visited Las Vegas, compared to 18 million visitors in 1989, when the "reinvention" of the city began at the Mirage.

Steve Wynn, who would be widely credited with starting the transformation of Las Vegas into a world-class resort destination, was born in New Haven, Connecticut in 1942, and graduated with a Bachelor of Arts degree in English Literature from the University of Pennsylvania. Wynn's reputation began in the 1970s, when he turned the downtown Golden Nugget, once known only as a "gambling

ABOVE: The Mirage Resort's popular Dolphin Habitat is home to Atlantic bottlenose dolphins and is the center-piece of an educational program developed with Clark County schools.

joint," into a four-star, four-diamond resort known for its elegant facilities and personal service.

Wynn and his wife, Elaine Farrell Pascal, had moved to Las Vegas from Maryland in 1967, when Wynn began his career in the gaming industry as an executive and part owner of the Frontier Hotel. In addition, between 1968 and 1972, he owned and operated a wine and liquor importing company in the state of Nevada. His dealings included a real estate transaction with Howard Hughes, the profits from which allowed him to begin a major investment in the Golden Nugget Casino on Fremont Street in 1972.

The Golden Nugget, which was licensed by the Nevada Gaming Commission in 1946, was the oldest established gaming company in the state. In August 1973, when Wynn took over, it was a small casino with no hotel rooms. Under his direction, the company commenced a major remodeling program to transform the Golden Nugget into a first-class destination resort. The result was a facility with 1,907 rooms and suites, 27 apartments, a spa, restaurants and, of course, the casino.

Wynn oversaw the building of the Golden Nugget Hotel and Casino on the Boardwalk in Atlantic City in 1980. This resort became known for its luxurious facilities, its innovative television advertising and superstar entertainment. Its sale to Bally's in 1987 for $440 million allowed Wynn the opportunity to focus his attention on the design and development of what would become the company's flagship property, the Mirage.

The Mirage opened on schedule in November 1989 at a total construction

OPPOSITE: The great Golden Nugget as it appeared in the early 1950s during the heyday of Glitter Gulch. It was the oldest established gaming company in the state when Steve Wynn acquired the property in 1973, but it was dwarfed by later developments. He completely revamped the Golden Nugget, adding hotel rooms and creating a major resort. Capitalizing on the classic mystique of the property, he even went so far as to create a Golden Nugget Hotel and Casino for the Boardwalk in Atlantic City.

RIGHT: One of the most amazing sights on the Strip each night is the eruption of the Mirage Resort's 54-foot volcano. Flames shoot into the sky and special lighting effects transform an otherwise tranquil waterfall into streams of molten lava. The eruptions, which occur on the quarter hour after dark, always draw a crowd of excited vacationers.

ABOVE: The grounds of the Mirage Resort are noted for multiple lagoons and waterfalls. The waterfall at right is transformed into a volcano after dark.

cost of $630 million. It went on to attain record levels of revenue for both the casino and non-casino operations. In fact, without counting the casino revenue, the Mirage has been calculated to be the most successful hotel in the history of the hospitality industry.

The Mirage introduced the concept of a complete destination resort, capturing the imaginations of its guests with its Polynesian motif, a nine-story atrium filled with palm trees and other South Seas-style horticulture. The tropical theme also features a five-acre front lagoon complete with a fire-erupting volcano, a tropical rain forest with waterfalls and lagoons, and a 20,000 gallon salt water aquarium behind the front desk. The Mirage has 3,049

hotel rooms and suites, meeting, convention and banquet space which can accommodate groups from five to 5,000 and a host of other amenities and public areas, all in keeping with its tropical theme. The vast casino is designed as a Polynesian village.

With its design reflecting the exotic romance of the tropics, the Mirage is home to two habitats for rare or endangered animals: royal white tigers and seven Atlantic bottlenose dolphins. While they provide great enjoyment for guests, the habitats also serve as educational centers for guests and schoolchildren throughout the Las Vegas community. The Mirage dolphin environment was one of Steve Wynn's dreams. He wanted to provide a

ABOVE: A tropical rain forest has been carefully recreated inside the Mirage Resort's 90-foot atrium. Featured flora includes palms, orchids, elephant ears and banana trees.

ABOVE: The Mirage Resort's registration desk is backed by a 20,000-gallon saltwater tank filled with exotic coral reef fish.

OPPOSITE: Siegfried, Roy and one of their royal white tigers are featured on the marquee of the Mirage Resort, which is located next door to the Forum Shops at Caesars Palace.

healthy and nurturing environment for dolphins and to increase the public's awareness and commitment to protecting while conserving marine mammals and their environment.

An educational program has been developed by the Mirage dolphin project staff and the Clark County School system to give students an opportunity to visit the Dolphin Habitat and learn about the mammals, as well as the fragility of marine ecology. In addition, the Dolphin Habitat offers community outreach programs such as lectures, workshops and special events on a regular basis. Specialists from around the world were asked to lend their expertise and ideas in order to create a safe, healthy and state-of-the-art facility. The size of the pools — 2.5 million gallons — exceeds government regulations by more than eight times. Furthermore, a commitment was made by the Mirage to display only dolphins already in captivi-

ABOVE: The royal white tigers who work with Siegfried and Roy are in residence in a public viewing area at the Mirage.

OPPOSITE: Siegfried and Roy are memorialized in bronze at Siegfried and Roy Plaza, a small cul-de-sac off Las Vegas Boulevard, north of Dauphine Way.

ty and that no dolphins will be taken from the wild for the habitat. Meanwhile, the Mirage's Royal White Tiger Habitat is home to the cats used in the show at the Mirage that features the world-famous entertainers and illusionists Siegfried and Roy.

If the Rat Pack epitomized Las Vegas style in the 1960s, and Elvis was the King of Las Vegas in the 1970s, then the crown and scepter certainly passed in the 1990s to Siegfried and Roy. They came to the Mirage in February 1990, after establishing a new Las Vegas record of six and one half years at the Frontier Hotel between 1981 and 1987. It was the longest-running hit show in Las Vegas history. In Japan, in 1988 they set an all-time attendance record during an eight-month live tour,

LEFT: Though they live in their own Dolphin Habitat on the opposite side of the property, the Mirage Resort's Atlantic bottlenose dolphins are celebrated in bronze in the lagoons that face Las Vegas Boulevard. The Dolphin Habitat offers community outreach programs such as lectures, workshops and special events on a regular basis. Specialists from around the world were asked to lend their expertise and ideas in order to create a safe, healthy and state-of-the-art facility. The 2.5 million gallon pools at the Dolphin Habitat exceed government regulation size by more than eight times.

ABOVE: Looking across the marquee of the Sands Hotel and Casino toward the Mirage Resort. For 44 years the Sands was one of the landmark properties on the Strip.

OPPOSITE: The Sands marquee as it appeared at the end of 1996. When the Sands was brought down, the marquee was the last to go, and the dry eyes were in a minority. The legendary Sands was founded in 1952 with the backing of Jack Entratter, who operated New York's Copacabana nightclub. The first headliner in the Copa Room at the Sands was Danny Thomas, but the room is perhaps best remembered as the scene of the Rat Pack's 1960 "Summit," which was attended by presidential candidate John F. Kennedy.

playing to more than one million people, while a year later they broke a 57 year record for attendance and gross receipts at New York's Radio City Music Hall. The duo are also two-time winners of the "Magicians of the Year" award from the Academy of Magical Arts in Los Angeles. In 1995, Siegfried and Roy marked their fifth anniversary at the Mirage Resort by setting an all-time Las Vegas box office record: Their act grossed more than a quarter of a billion dollars in five years. Also in 1995, Siegfried and Roy won the "Liberace Legend Award" from the Liberace Foundation for the Performing and Creative Arts.

They were both born in Germany, with Siegfried taking an early interest in magic, and Roy with animals. Combining their talents into a night club show, the pair achieved international acclaim after a performance at Monte Carlo's Sporting Club for Prince Rainier and Princess Grace.

Today, Siegfried and Roy make their home in Las Vegas, with tigers roaming the grounds almost as if they were regular house pets. Their professional home is the $25 million Siegfried and Roy Theater built for them at the Mirage by Steve Wynn. They are quite active in conservation projects, including efforts to save the near-extinct white lions of Timbavati.

The Tiger Habitat at the Mirage contains many features designed to enhance the comfort of the animals and provide spectacular viewing for guests. The open air environment features a swimming pool with fountains and simulated mountain terrain for the tiger's enjoyment and the public's entertainment. The facility's white setting gives the animals a sense of security by allowing them to blend into the background and special slanted glass affords better viewing, eliminates glare and helps control the temperature.

The royal white tigers are rotated continuously in and out of the facility throughout the day. When not appearing in the Habitat, they enjoy their own spacious living environment and periodic excursions into the surrounding Nevada desert.

Other casinos on the Strip have continued to open new properties to meet the expectations and

OPENED
DEC. 15, 1952

44 GREAT YEARS

THANK YOU

ABOVE: The famous Circus Circus clown marquee has been inviting friends of all ages since the property opened in 1968. A new 35-story tower was added in 1997.

needs of vacationers. In 1988, 20 years after it opened its family-oriented, circus-themed casino, Circus Circus Enterprises acquired a 117-acre site on the southwest corner of Las Vegas Boulevard South and Tropicana Avenue. The company announced plans for what would be the world's largest hotel/casino with two 28-story towers totaling 4,032 rooms. Ground-breaking ceremonies for the new property, dubbed Excalibur, took place on October 7, 1988, in a setting of medieval pageantry, complete with richly-gowned ladies-in-waiting and a display of jousting by mounted knights in armor.

According to legend, Excalibur was a magical sword embedded in stone. During a period of unrest and disunity in post-Roman Britain, it was proclaimed that whomever could pull the sword from the stone would be crowned King of England. After knights of high renown failed in their attempts to free the sword, Arthur, a mere squire, succeeded. King Arthur's reign gave birth to the tales of Camelot. The Knights of the Round Table and the Arthurian legend form the basis for much of the resort's plush decor.

After 20 months of construction, the long-awaited Castle opened its doors in June 1990. Ribbon-cutting ceremonies were conducted with the assistance of Jack D. and Betty Houston of Knoxville, Tennessee, the winners of an international "Name the Castle" contest. Trumpeters, fireworks, and a release of 15,000 red, white and blue balloons let the whole city know Excalibur was ready for business. An estimated 30,000 guests visited the castle-themed resort within the first few hours of operation.

In addition to accommodations and over 100,000 square feet of gaming, Excalibur features two swimming pools, six marvelous restaurants, the King Arthur's Tournament dinner show, afternoon performances of "An Evening in Vienna" by the Royal Lipizzaner Stallions and two magic motion simulator theaters.

King Arthur's Tournament, a performance unlike any other in Las Vegas, takes place in a 900-seat arena, where the audience becomes an intricate part of the show. Laser lighting and special effects such as fireworks and clouds of billowing water vapor give the production an air of mystery and magic. Audiences are treated to a very realistic joust and bat-

ABOVE: The Strip by night with Harrah's at center stage. The river boat was deleted in 1996. Behind Harrah's is the Flamingo Hilton. The Sands is in the lower left, and Excalibur can be seen in the distance at top right.

BELOW: The Strip, circa 1996, looking north, with the Sands at the center, and Harrah's on the right.

ABOVE: Entering the Excalibur Hotel and Casino is like entering a Medieval castle.

OPPOSITE: The Excalibur's showroom features King Arthur's Tournament, an actual jousting tournament in which mounted knights square off in a 900-seat arena. The White Knight always defeats the treacherous Dark Knight to win a princess' hand in marriage.

tle scene conducted by stuntmen on horseback with metal swords and axes. The story begins when Merlin the Magician grants a young boy's wish to be a knight by transporting him back to the Middle Ages and transforming him into the White Knight of Kent, the hero of this musical drama. During his adventures the White Knight meets King Arthur and Queen Guinevere, then battles the treacherous Dark Knight, and wins a princess' hand in marriage.

Award-winning French designer Michel Fresnay lent his hand to the production, creating costumes which accurately reflect the style of the Middle Ages.

Fresnay's talents produced knights dressed in lavish, embroidered satin tunics with authentic coats of arms, dancing maidens garbed in the spectacular glittering bodices and skirts, and a mystical Merlin frocked in a glorious flowing robe of midnight blue.

The most dynamic element of this production is the show's producer and creator, Peter Jackson.

ABOVE: King Arthur's Tournament at the Excalibur features mounted stuntmen with replicas of real Medieval hardware and weaponry.

LEFT: The Excalibur at night is a spectacular sight. No castle in Medieval times ever benefitted by lighting this dramatic.

ABOVE: At the 1994 VIP New Year's Eve party at the Excalibur, entertainer Robert Goulet was knighted by "Merlin," the sorcerer to the court of the Excalibur's "King Arthur."

OPPOSITE: The famous Lipizzaner stallions perform in the Excalibur's "An Evening in Vienna" show. The Lipizzaners are specially bred for show at the Spanish Riding School in Vienna, Austria.

Jackson and his son, co-producer Patrick Jackson, are completely dedicated to the success of this production, which is sold out nearly every performance, six years running.

The Lipizzaners' performance of "An Evening in Vienna" showcases the stallions' superior ability, intelligence, and beauty. Resulting from careful crossbreeding, Lipizzaners are a breed of horse that is primarily a mix of the Spanish Andalusian, the Arabian, and the swift and sturdy Karst of the Adriatic coast. This crossbreeding created the perfect animal to present the elegant and graceful movements of dressage, a classical horse training tradition. The precise and exacting principles of dressage were first defined in Greece in 400 BC. Following the fall of the Greek empire, the principles sank into oblivion until they were rediscovered in Italy in the seventeenth century. The rediscovery of dressage, especially "haute ecole," or advanced training, caused a sensation in aristocratic Europe. For the first time since ancient Greece, the horse was being presented not as a common beast of burden or to carry soldiers, but as a living work of art, a creature to be enjoyed solely for its grace, beauty, and power. Historically, the horses were bred and raised by the emperors of Austria on an exclusive estate which only a privileged few were permitted to visit, and were often reserved as special gifts for select friends, making them highly prized possessions. With their noble bearing, impressive white coats, and powerful builds, these horses were an excellent match for the imposing surroundings of the most splendid Spanish Riding School in Vienna. Today, there are only two performing units of Lipizzaners in the world outside of the famous Vienna school.

In October 1993, Mirage Resorts opened the $475 million pirate-themed resort, Treasure Island,

ABOVE: Treasure Island's marquee certainly catches one's attention.

OPPOSITE: Treasure Island's "Battle of Buccaneer Bay" provides the most stunning pyrotechnic show on the Strip.

which has been described as "an idyllic pirate getaway, based upon the village created by Robert Louis Stevenson in his famed novel, *Treasure Island.*" The 36-story Treasure Island is located adjacent to the Mirage on the Las Vegas Strip and features 2,900 rooms, including 212 suites. All of Treasure Island's public areas maintain the theme of an eighteenth century pirate village built of pieces of the booty and plunder that pirates might have captured throughout the years.

The resort is famous for featuring a "live" sea battle between full-scale replicas of the pirate ship *Hispaniola* and the British frigate, HMS *Britannia*, which are anchored in the lagoon in front of the property. The battle's climax includes the complete destruction and sinking of the nearly 100-foot-long British frigate.

The sea battle takes place at Treasure Island's signature location, Buccaneer Bay, a spectacular facade at the front of the property where the *Hispaniola* is docked unloading a cache of ill-gotten goods. Every 90 minutes, the British frigate sails around Skull Point to confront the pirate ship.

The pyrotechnic battle ensues as cannon and musket fire are exchanged and some of the stunt people are thrown from their ships into the water. The pirates, appearing to be losing the battle, make one last ditch effort to fire their cannon at the British. The pirate captain swings across the ship from the bow to the stern, grabs a smoldering ember and lights the fuse on the final cannon. The fateful shot hits the *Britannia* dead center.

The *Britannia* tilts to one side and slowly sinks into the waters below as the British captain stands defiantly on deck and goes down with his ship. As

ABOVE: The Plank at Treasure Island offers fine dining in a setting designed to simulate the library of an urbane pirate captain. Artifacts in the cases suggest possible plunder.

Treasure Island's press release puts it "After all, this is Las Vegas. The pirates always win."

Treasure Island's casino maintains the feel of an old Caribbean pirate hideaway, and the property also features two graciously appointed wedding chapels created in an elegant European style with marble-lined altars and exquisite floral arrangements.

Set amid intimate surroundings, one chapel seats 60 guests and the other accommodates 30. A professional bridal consultant assigned to each wedding assists in all the arrangements, including reception planning, formal wear rental and securing the officiant to perform the ceremony.

"We wanted to provide our guests with elegant surroundings in an exciting setting where they could get married or renew their vows," said Tina

Ercole, the wedding chapel manager. "The Treasure Island wedding chapels offer couples all the personalized service imaginable to make their special day just perfect."

The world-renowned French Canadian performing troupe Cirque du Soleil makes its North American home at Treasure Island's 1,500-seat theater. Cirque du Soleil officially debuted in Quebec in 1984 as part of the 450th anniversary celebration of Jacques Cartier's discovery of the country that came to be known as Canada. Encouraged by its initial success, Cirque went on a 50-performance tour of 11 cities in Quebec.

The Cirque du Soleil Big Top grew from 800 to 1,500 seats as Cirque expanded its tour of Canada in 1985 and 1986, including a dazzling performance at Expo '86 in Vancouver.

ABOVE: The elegant registration lobby at Treasure Island features gilt chandeliers. A portion of Captain Morgan's Lounge is visible at the left.

In 1987, Cirque du Soleil toured the United States with shows in Los Angeles, San Diego and Santa Monica. The performances drew capacity crowds and glowing reviews, prompting the Montreal-based touring company to expand its 1988 tour to include New York City (where the Big Top stood in the shadow of the World Trade Center) and Washington DC. In 1989, the troupe visited Miami, Chicago and Phoenix, and received its first Emmy in the "Outstanding Special Event" category for the HBO presentation of "The Magic Circus."

Cirque du Soleil's relationship with Las Vegas dates back to 1992, when Mirage Resorts Incorporated entered into partnership with the Montreal-based touring troupe. Cirque's production of *Nouvelle Experience* played for a year under the yellow-and-white Big Top at the Mirage, before then taking up residence at Treasure Island with the show *Mystere.* "Cirque is the ideal complement to Treasure Island," said Steve Wynn. "Our international guests find Cirque to be a special delight with no language or cultural barriers. People from all over the world enjoy the wonder and pleasure to be found at a Cirque performance."

ABOVE: The Treasure Island Buffet features an Oriental motif.

OPPOSITE : From the windows in Treasure Island's Buccaneer Bay Club, one can watch the nightly "Battle of Buccaneer Bay" unfold with its explosive fury.

ABOVE: This detail view of the pirate ship *Hispaniola*, anchored in Treasure Island's Buccaneer Bay, shows the level of craftsmanship that went into recreating the vessel.

ABOVE: Treasure Island's HMS *Britannia* is rigged in full sail, because in the Battle of Buccaneer Bay she sails in to do battle with the pirates.

ABOVE: A bit worse for wear after all its years, the Blue Angel is not counted among the great Las Vegas "theme" properties, but it does evoke a mood and a sense of another era.

RIGHT: The Normandie on Las Vegas Boulevard defines its theme in three words. On his first visit to Las Vegas the King was not yet the King, and the Normandie afforded him what we hope was a good night's sleep. The reverse of the sign carries an authoritative recommendation for the Normandie, from its owner.

Redefining the Classics

During the 1990s, Las Vegas would experience a renaissance, as the classic properties renewed themselves and introduced the new features that would keep them forever young. From the changes on the Strip, to the amazing Fremont Street Experience, plenty new was in the air.

During the 1990s, many of the classic properties built in the 1950s and 1960s brushed up their images and reinvented themselves in order to keep pace with the rapid changes going on in Las Vegas. In June 1990, the 36-year-old Showboat Hotel, Casino and Bowling Center unveiled what was the largest four-color, animated, electronic sign in the United States. The electronic face of the Showboat Marquee is 30 feet by 80 feet, with 36,000 bulbs — making that portion of the sign nearly twice as large as any other electronic marquee in Las Vegas.

"Research has shown there's nothing even close to the size of the Showboat sign in the United States," said Bill Fain of Sign Systems, builder of the marquee. "It might even be the largest in the world." Components for the computer-generated sign were made in Canada, Seattle and Las Vegas, while most of the stationary structure was manufactured at the Sign Systems Las Vegas warehouse. Construction of the eleven-story marquee was part of a multi-million dollar renovation that included construction of the all-new Bingo Gardens, two new specialty restaurants, a five-story covered parking garage, and a new front entrance.

Throughout the 1990s, Bally's Las Vegas underwent an extensive remodeling program in which improvements were made to nearly every aspect of the resort. Opened in 1973, Bally's Las Vegas has been considered one of the city's most elegant resorts, offering its guests "a touch of class" in every aspect of service. The distinctive resort encompasses more than 3.2 million square feet of public space and two 26-story hotel towers which offer 2,814 guest rooms, including 265 suites.

The 2,700-room Imperial Palace on the Strip is perhaps best known for its Antique and Classic Auto Collection, which includes many of the world's rarest, most exotic automobiles. There are more than 800 automobiles in the collection, with over 200 on display at any one time, including cars owned and driven by stars which range from Tom

ABOVE: When country star Lynn Anderson headlined at the Showboat in 1996, it evoked the roots that Las Vegas still has in the rich history of the American West.

ABOVE: Because it is, after all, the desert, most Las Vegas properties offer patrons a pool. These vacationers are enjoying their tropical beverages at the Lady Luck.

RIGHT: When it was installed in 1990, the Showboat's marquee was the largest four-color, animated, electronic sign in the United States. It stands eight stories tall and includes 36,000 bulbs.

ABOVE (BOTH): Included in the Imperial Palace Auto Collection is Marilyn Monroe's coral pink 1955 Lincoln Capri convertible. When the car was acquired by the Imperial Palace in 1993, it had only 26,000 miles on the odometer.

Mix to Marilyn Monroe. The 1976 Cadillac Eldorado once owned by Elvis Presley is on display, as are several cars that belonged to Liberace. These include his famous customized 1981 Zimmer Golden Spirit as well as his gold-trimmed 1966 Rolls Royce Silver Shadow. The 1930 Cadillac originally owned by Al Capone is also on view. It was heavily armored and had a system for creating a smoke screen. An important part of the collection features cars used by important historical figures. Visitors can view the cars of every American president from Roosevelt to Nixon, and those used by the infamous 1940s fascist dictators Benito Mussolini and Adolf Hitler.

Also at the Imperial Palace is the stage show "Legends in Concert," a live, on-stage recreation of the performances of a select group of superstars from the past and present. The talented performers not only sound like the original stars — no lip-syncing here — but they also look and perform

like them, as well. Included are impersonators of John Lennon, Marilyn Monroe, Judy Garland, Nat King Cole, Cher, Elton John, Michael Jackson, Madonna, the Beatles, Liberace, Dolly Parton and the Blues Brothers, all backed by singer-dancers and a live band. The shows typically close with a tribute to Elvis Presley and an encore in which the Elvis impersonator leads the entire cast in a heart-stopping rendition of "Viva Las Vegas."

Another of the older hotels that redefined itself during the 1990s was the hotel which opened in 1969 as the International and became the Las Vegas Hilton two years later.

With 3,174 luxurious rooms and suites, the 30-story Las Vegas Hilton is set on 80 lush, land-scaped acres. The lobby features solid glass walls accented by a 16 foot glass and brass revolving door, marble floors, and imported crystal chande-liers. Elegantly appointed with marble, rich woods

ABOVE: A highlight of the Imperial Palace Auto Collection is Liberace's gold-trimmed 1966 Rolls-Royce Silver Shadow. The entertainer actually used it as his "around town" car when he was in residence at his Las Vegas home.

ABOVE: The expansive Las Vegas Hilton is situated on Paradise Road, one block east of the Strip.

RIGHT: Andrew Lloyd Webber's Starlight Express has been featured at the Las Vegas Hilton since 1993. In custom designing a theater for Starlight Express," the Las Vegas Hilton had created a room that was perfect for musicians and other performers. While the Starlight Theater can seat 1,572 patrons for Starlight Express," it can accommodate 1,728 for Fabulous Fridays because many of the production show's skating runways are not necessary.

ABOVE: Popular for their lively 1950s-style review, the music and dance ensemble, Sha Na Na have made numerous appearances in Las Vegas, notably at the Showboat.

OPPOSITE: The view from the long driveway leading into the Las Vegas Hilton complex from Paradise Road.

and tier after tier of imported crystal, the Las Vegas Hilton's 67,000-square-foot casino is one of the world's most prestigious gaming facilities. A game for every preference is offered 24 hours a day. baccarat, blackjack (21), craps, roulette, Big Six Wheel, keno, pai cow, pai cow poker, mini-baccarat, Let It Ride and Caribbean stud, along with slot machines, video poker and other coin machines in every denomination can all be found on the casino floor. Slot players can win additional cash and gift certificates by joining the free Club Magic slot club. The renowned Las Vegas Hilton race and sports SuperBook® is a high-tech wonderland for the sports enthusiast.

This impressive 30,500-square-foot facility is the largest of its kind in the world, featuring more than 40 video screens and the most technologically advanced audiovisual systems to be found any-

ABOVE: A happy couple celebrates in the Winner's Cafe at the Lady Luck Casino. They are obviously winners, and right at home here

LEFT: A view of the Strip from the grounds of the Stardust. The Stratosphere, the tallest structure in Las Vegas, is visible in the center, and the Silver City and Riviera can be seen across the Strip. El Rancho was undergoing its transformation into the Starship Orion when this photograph was taken.

ABOVE: Jeff Kutash's fabulous review, Splash, had its debut in the Versailles Theatre at the Riviera in 1985. The show evolved into Splash II, whose staging is seen here in 1996.

where. Its solid wall of video is second in size only to that maintained by NASA's mission control.

The elegant Las Vegas Hilton Showroom showcased the world's top superstars for nearly a quarter-century before becoming the futuristic Starlight Theater, the North American home of Andrew Lloyd Webber's Starlight Express in 1993. Superstars who had appeared in the former Hilton Showroom were headliners such as Elvis Presley, Barbra Streisand (the room's first headliner), Liberace, Bill Cosby, Wayne Newton, Engelbert Humperdink, Tony Orlando, Ann-Margaret, Glen Campbell, and Gladys Knight, who was the last entertainer to perform before the showroom was rebuilt.

Recently, the Las Vegas Hilton has been bringing entertainers into the Starlight Theater on selected Friday nights, when Starlight Express is dark.

"It was absolutely a natural," said Foster Wilson, Las Vegas Hilton vice president of entertainment. "One day, Gary Gregg (president of the hotel) and I were in the Starlight Theater standing on the 'bowl' that serves as the center stage for Starlight Express. We were talking about the seat configuration of the showroom, with its theater-style seating, and the light and sound systems, considered to be the best in Las Vegas. All of a sudden a light bulb went off, and we knew we had a great idea. Why not bring name entertainment in on 'Starlight's' night off?"

Ironically, in custom designing a home for Starlight Express, the Las Vegas Hilton had created a theater that was perfect for musicians and other performers. "Everything our entertainers needed was already in place and set up," said Gary Gregg. "No other venue is so ideally suited for every type of act. When sound, lighting, space, and the fact that every seat in the house is a good one are all combined, our Starlight Theater provides the finest amenities in Las Vegas for any performer."

While the room can seat 1,572 patrons for Starlight Express, it can accommodate 1,728 for Fabulous Fridays because many of the production show's skating runways are not necessary.

Acts booked into the Starlight Theater include Creedence Clearwater Revisited (formerly Creedence Clearwater Revival), country/western singer Lorrie Morgan, political satirist/comedian Bill Maher, Ramsey Lewis, Lou Rawls, the Monkees 39th Anniversary Tour, the sensational jazz combo of Michael Franks with Boney James, Johnny Cash and the June Carter Family, Al Jarreau, a disco reunion featuring K.C. and the Sunshine Band, Rose Royce, Thelma Houston and Peaches and Herb.

Perhaps no one sums up the entire Fabulous Fridays/Starlight Theater experience better than jazz vocalist Nancy Wilson, a veteran performer in the Hilton Showroom.

When shown the completely rebuilt Starlight Theater, Wilson exclaimed, "I can't believe it. It's really cute! We tried rock and roll, country, jazz, comedy, and they all worked. Every Fabulous Fridays act receives standing ovations, with no exceptions. The theater's set-up is perfect for entertainer/audience communication, whereby the entertainer can easily mingle with the audience. It's an up-close and personal situation."

ABOVE: The Riviera has been a mecca for entertainment-lovers since Liberace opened the Clover Room on April 20, 1955. The current showroom, the Versailles, opened in 1960.

ABOVE AND OPPOSITE: The Flamingo Hilton has the longest history of any of the Strip casinos. It dates back to the 105-room Flamingo, opened by Bugsy Siegel in 1946, before Las Vegas Boulevard was known as the Strip. Now a Hilton, the property has changed considerably. It now has over 3,600 rooms and it recently underwent a $130 million upgrade and expansion.

Conventions have also utilized the Starlight Theater for their own shows; television specials such as the "Academy Awards of Sports" and the Victor Awards have also been taped there. In 1997, the Las Vegas Hilton opened "Star Trek, the Experience," a joint project between Hilton Hotels Corporation and Paramount Parks.

With over 220,000 square feet of meeting space and almost next door to the Las Vegas Convention Center, the Las Vegas Hilton is the world's single largest convention hotel. The entire meeting and convention area is equipped with technically superior lighting, audio and visual features. Such major conventions as the Consumer Electronics Show, COMDEX, the National Association of Broadcasters and International Council of Shopping Centers meet regularly at the Las Vegas Hilton.

In 1994, Caesars Palace was purchased by ITT Corporation and the following year, the property expanded with the addition of the $25 million, eight story theme complex called "Caesars Magical Empire." One entrance at Caesars Palace now serves as a principal gateway to the Forum Shops At Caesars, a $100 million, 240,000 square foot lavish shopping center that opened May 1, 1992. Storefronts and common areas in the mall resemble an ancient Roman street, with immense columns and arches, central piazzas, ornate fountains and classic statuary that continues the theme started in Caesars Palace. Overhead, the vaulted ceiling features a changing sky, emulating the ambiance of a Mediterranean evening.

While rapid changes were happening on the Strip in the 1980s and early 1990s, the old downtown area around Fremont Street was slipping into

ABOVE: Singer Sheryl Crow at the time of her 1993 appearance at the Showboat's Carnival Room. Popular with Las Vegas audiences, she was invited to be an opening act at the Hard Rock Casino in 1995.

decline. In 1994, a major effort began to rejuvenate the area under a project that would create a four-block pedestrian mall. Fremont Street was permanently closed to automobile traffic on September 7, 1994, soon to be transformed into a towering ninety foot tall, four block long "space frame," with its 2.1 million light bulbs and 540 kilowatt state-of-the-art sound system. The Fremont Street Experience, the cornerstone for the comprehensive redevelopment of downtown Las Vegas, was a private and public partnership between the Fremont Street Experience Company — owned by a group of downtown casino operators — and the City of Las Vegas.

ABOVE: One of the most popular recent Las Vegas films was the 1992 Castle Rock Entertainment release *Honeymoon in Vegas.* In the film, Nicholas Cage (right) brings his fiance, played by Sara Jessica Parker (center), to Las Vegas. Their plan is to get married, but Cage runs afoul of tough-talking high roller Tommy Korman, played by James Caan (left).

LEFT: After four decades as an important cornerstone of Fremont Street, the Golden Nugget is one of the landmarks of the new Fremont Street Experience.

Toward the New Millennium

With major theme properties opening on the average of one or two a year, the face of Las Vegas is changing, but the mood and the excitement remain the same. Las Vegas is the city that never sleeps, a place where the gaming floors operate seamlessly all day and all night, day after day, night after night.

By the end of the twentieth century, Las Vegas moved toward the millennium — and its own centennial — as more than a vacation resort and a mecca for gaming. The elaborate theme properties had made the city itself a place to see and experience.

Opened on October 15, 1993 and built at a cost of $375 million, the Luxor Hotel-Casino is one of the most striking theme properties on the Strip. Built by Circus Circus Enterprises, the resort is named after the Egyptian city in upper Egypt. Inside the 30-story, pyramid-shaped hotel are reproductions of artifacts from Luxor and Karnak Temple as well as a full-scale reproduction of King Tut's Tomb. Throughout the pyramid, artists have painted authentic copies of hieroglyphics found in the Valley of the Kings and Valley of the Queens. An astonishing central atrium of 29 million cubic feet soars to the apex of the pyramid. Also inside are seven theme restaurants, an action ride based on technology similar to that used in flight simulators,

a simulated chase inside the pyramid and an oval arena showroom.

Guests enter the Luxor beneath a massive sphinx and lasers lance from the eyes of the statue to create figures and scenes against water spraying from a lavish fountain in front of the hotel. Barges on the Luxor's River Nile, which is five times longer than the height of the 350-foot pyramid, give guests a 15 minute tour around the perimeter of the resort's casino. Luxor's elevators, called "inclinators," travel at a 39-degree angle up the slope of the structure. The world's most powerful beam of light shines from the top of the pyramid. The light is so bright that it is visible to airplanes flying over Los Angeles, 250 miles away.

Opened on December 18, 1993, the billion-dollar MGM Grand Hotel, Casino and Theme Park was built by MGM Grand Incorporated, whose principal owner is the visionary developer and entrepreneur Kirk Kerkorian. The 112-acre resort hotel, casino and Hollywood image theme park is

ABOVE: One of the Luxor's limousines rests in the shadow of the palms near the resort's signature sphinx.

ABOVE: The interior of the Luxor's fabled black pyramid is an ancient Egypt-themed wonderland that is visible from the entrances to the rooms.

RIGHT: The Luxor's black pyramid is the resort's dominant structure, but the sphinx and other replicas of Egyptian statuary are certainly eye-catching.

the largest entertainment resort of its kind, and the largest hotel-casino in the world. The resort has eight theme restaurants, two main showrooms, spas, pools, four lighted tennis courts, a "youth hotel" and a 15,200-seat special events arena. The 33-acre movie lot theme park features 10 food and beverage locations, 12 major attractions, theme streets, four theaters, and other attractions that feature a Cotton Blossom Riverboat, Ghost Coaster, Journey to the Center of the Earth (a motion machine), French Bumper Cars, a haunted silver mine and more.

The Grand Adventures theme park is located on 33 acres of land on the north side of the hotel-casino that has a studio backlot theme with

ABOVE: The MGM Grand's signature lion dwarfs all around him. He presides over a vast complex with over 4,200 rooms.

seven rides, five shows and eight themed streets. Included are a backlot river tour with a war scene and a Huey helicopter, Grand Canyon Rapids, a free-flow boat ride and Over the Edge, a log flume ride. Interestingly, the water for these attractions is pulled from underground wells owned by MGM. Indoor rides include the Lightning Bolt, a roller coaster that is 50 percent faster that Disneyland's Space Mountain.

Billing itself as "the world's first — and only — rock n' roll hotel," the plush 11-story Hard Rock Hotel and Casino opened three blocks east of the Strip on Paradise Road in the pre-dawn hours of March 9, 1995. A star-studded celebration on March 10 and 11 featured the Eagles and Sheryl

ABOVE: The MGM Grand by night is a cool green, which reflects the Wizard of Oz theme that runs through the resort.

ABOVE: The early morning sun tints the Luxor's 10-story sphinx with an aura of mystery.

RIGHT: The Luxor's stunning 30-story bronze pyramid and two recently-added pyramid-shaped towers give the resort a total of nearly 4,000 guest rooms.

ABOVE: With a nine-story Fender Stratocaster as its facade, it is hard to miss the Hard Rock Casino. Inside are actual guitars that once belonged to Nirvana, Bruce Springsteen and Eric Clapton.

Crow, who flew in for the occasion. As with the Hard Rock Cafes that exist in various cities around the world, the property is filled with hundreds of thousands of dollars worth of rock music memorabilia, including Pearl Jam's surfboard, a guitar used by Nirvana, James Brown's gold jacket, and guitars once owned by Elvis Presley, Chris Isaak, Tom Petty and Depeche Mode. Glass kiosks house musical instruments and costumes worn by such stars as "the Artist Formerly Known As Prince."

The centerpiece of the Hard Rock property is the 30,000-square-foot casino where the color-coded gaming chips carry the image of specific rock performers. For example, the red $5 chips carry a Red Hot Chili Peppers picture, while the

purple $25 chips are Jimi Hendrix "Purple Haze" chips. The $100 Tom Petty is the "You Got Lucky" chip. Roulette wheels spin in mock pianos and the blackjack tables are adorned with lyrics from famous rock songs. Harvey's, the firm that owns and operates Harvey's Hotel and Casino at Lake Tahoe, manages the Hard Rock's casino.

The diverse calendar of acts performing in the Hard Rock's 1,200-seat "the Joint" showroom have ranged from the Black Crowes to Sheryl Crow, and have also included Steely Dan, Tracy Chapman, No Doubt, Coolio, Ted Nugent, Al Green, Lyle Lovett, Jimmy Cliff, Boz Scaggs, the Gipsy Kings, Weird Al Yankovic, Spin Doctors, Joe Satriani, Eric Johnson, Keith Sweat, Social Distortion, Merle

ABOVE: The memorabilia collection at the Hard Rock Hotel and Casino includes Elvis Presley's gold jacket, as well as Las Vegas hotel menus autographed both by Elvis and by Jimi Hendrix.

RIGHT: Opened in 1996, the Monte Carlo Resort and Casino is renown for its Corinthian detailing and its recreation of the atmosphere of a nineteenth century Mediterranean resort such as one might have encountered in the city of Monte Carlo. With more than 2,700 rooms, its huge casino floor and other facilities, the Monte Carlo in Las Vegas is almost as large as the city for which it is named.

ABOVE: Gleaming copper fermenting tanks shimmer in the Monte Carlo's Pub and Brewery. The Monte Carlo was the first casino resort in Las Vegas to produce its own beer on its premises.

OPPOSITE: The level of detail that was used in creating the Monte Carlo's Las Vegas Boulevard entrance creates a mood of sophistication.

Haggard, Neal McCoy, Ratdog, Santana, Hootie and the Blowfish, as well as Crosby, Stills and Nash.

Meanwhile, Circus Circus Enterprises and Mirage Resorts collaborated on a $344 million project, a joint venture called the Monte Carlo Resort and Casino. This property opened on June 21, 1996, amid fireworks and a performance by the soon-to-be house star, Lance Burton, Master Magician. The Monte Carlo features a 90,000 square feet of casino space, including a full service Race and Sports Book, and the 1,200 seat showroom known as the Lance Burton Theater. The Monte Carlo was also the first Las Vegas Resort to include a brewpub among its six restaurants.

The tallest casino in Las Vegas is the Stratosphere Las Vegas, which opened in 1996. Standing 1,149 feet, the Stratosphere Tower is America's tallest free-standing observation tower

ABOVE: While the Monte Carlo was the first hotel and casino to have a brewpub, the whimsical Holy Cow was the first brewpub in Las Vegas that was also a casino.

OPPOSITE: Looking north on the Strip toward Downtown Las Vegas and the Stratosphere. Opened in 1996, the Stratosphere is 1,149 feet tall.

and the tallest building west of the Mississippi River. A 12-story pod atop the tower features meeting rooms, a revolving restaurant and lounge, indoor and outdoor observation decks, and two of the most exciting thrill rides in the world — the Big Shot and the High Roller roller coaster. The Big Shot is a state-of-the-art ride located on the 113th floor that sends patrons 160 feet into the air before letting them fall back down to the launching pad. Located on the 112th floor, the High Roller is the world's highest roller coaster, making two clockwise rotations, banking sharply at 32-degree angles, and travelling at speeds up to 35 miles per hour.

ABOVE: By night, the "skyline" of the New York New York Hotel and Casino looks similar to the city for which it is named.

OPPOSITE: For people from New York City, it is strange to see the New York New York replica of their city on a Nevada street corner. The complex is surrounded by a roller coaster ride.

A thousand feet below the thrill rides, the Stratosphere Hotel and Casino opened with 1,500 rooms and suites, a 100,000 square foot World's Fair-themed casino, an international retail shopping mall called the Tower Shops at Stratosphere, and seven theme restaurants. An additional 1,000 rooms and suites and a spa and pool facility were added in 1996, and were soon joined by an 80,000 square foot aquarium with 360-degree views the following year. Feature entertainment included the American Superstar celebrity impersonator show with tributes to Madonna, Diana Ross and the Supremes, Michael Jackson, Gloria Estefan, the Temptations and Charlie Daniels.

One of the most talked-about — especially on the east coast — properties to open in Las Vegas in the 1990s was the New York New York Hotel and Casino. New York New York officially opened on January 3, 1997, with a VIP/celebrity "pre-open-

RIGHT: It is like Manhattan in the desert. In the New York New York complex, visitors can spend the night inside replicas of the Empire State Building, the Chrysler Building and other New York City landmarks. The Statue of Liberty does not, however, have guest rooms.

ABOVE AND OPPOSITE: The floor of the New York New York Casino carries the theme of the exterior of the complex. The vast casino encompasses 84,000 square feet. It contains 2,400 slot machines and 71 gaming tables.

ing" and fireworks January 2, 1997. A joint effort by MGM Grand, Incorporated and Primadonna Resorts, New York New York is a $460 million, 2,120-room hotel and casino that recreates replicas of many traditional New York City landmarks. Foremost is a 150-foot (one-half scale) Statue of Liberty that was constructed at the corner of Tropicana and Las Vegas Boulevard, framed by a backdrop of the hotel, whose vast facade was designed to give the impression of a mass of midtown Manhattan skyscrapers. Also included was a roller coaster which circled the entire property, including part of the interior of the casino, and which was intended to pay tribune to the legendary roller coaster at Coney Island.

RIGHT: The registration area at the New York New York is a masterpiece of Art Deco design and fine woodworking. The Art Deco theme recalls the design of New York City's Empire State Building, Chrysler Building and Rockefeller Center. Art Deco styling was used throughout the New York New York property from the elevator lobbies to the popular Empire Bar.

ABOVE: The high-tech Las Vegas Hilton race and sports SuperBook® is the largest of its kind in the world, featuring more than 40 video screens and the most technologically advanced systems to be found anywhere. Its solid wall of video is second in size only to that maintained by NASA's mission control.

The New York-skyline hotel towers include the AT&T Building and the Century Building, flanked by replicas of the art deco Empire State and Chrysler buildings. The miniature of the Empire State Building stands 48 stories and measures 525 feet, compared with 102 stories and 1,250 feet for the original.

With major theme properties opening on the average of one or two a year in the 1990s, the face of Las Vegas is changing rapidly, but the mood and the excitement remain the same. Las Vegas became the fastest growing city in the United States during the 1990s, but it has been attracting sophisticated visitors since the 1950s. It is the city that never sleeps, a place where the gaming floors operate seamlessly all day and all night, day after day, night after night.

Some people arrive on budget bus tours to spend a couple of rolls of quarters and see a show. Others fly in aboard private jets, rent limousines and play in cozy private rooms where the stakes on a single hand may be more than most visitors will earn in a year. Fortunes are won and lost in Las Vegas. Some who arrive in private jets leave as hitch-hikers along the hot and dusty US 95. Yet it is the uncertain promise, a promise not infrequently delivered upon, that draws people back.

Just as the land speaks of something eternal and enduring, the city itself is enduring. As old properties are bulldozed, they are quickly forgotten and promptly replaced by properties which are vastly more exciting and glamorous.

Just as the high desert speaks through the color of the sunlight on shifting sands and the moonlight on the shadows of the rocks, Las Vegas speaks through its dazzling shows and through its millions upon millions of light bulbs that flash and twinkle to create a brilliant and shimmering cityscape in that desert.

ABOVE: The tables at Binion's Horseshoe on Fremont Street offer friendly games and the highest stakes in town in a 50,000-square-foot casino.

LEFT: Since 1995, Fremont Street has been the Fremont Street Experience. The historic Pioneer is still visible on the left, and Jackie Gaughan's Plaza can be seen at the head of the street. A renovation costing $70 million has turned Glitter Gulch into a five-block pedestrian mall capped with a 90-foot steel mesh Celestial Vault. This covering provides shade in the daytime, and at night, its 2.1 million bulbs are a fascinating show.

ABOVE: Enjoying the spin of the roulette wheel at the
Lady Luck Casino. The 30,000-square-foot Lady Luck is
located a block north of Fremont Street on Third.

RIGHT: In 1946, Benny Binion staked his claim to the
Eldorado and renamed it the Horseshoe. Always a
Glitter Gulch landmark, today it is a cornerstone of the
Fremont Street Experience.

ABOVE: A perfect dream date in Las Vegas includes a yellow rose for the lady and for both, the excitement of the crap table at the Lady Luck Casino.

LEFT: The lights and excitement of Glitter Gulch, now the Fremont Street Experience. A neon Elvis impersonator smiles from the marquee at Sassy Sally's.

ABOVE: Looking west along Fremont Street in the years before Glitter Gulch became the Fremont Street Experience. The street was still open to traffic.

RIGHT: The marquee at the Four Queens has been spruced up considerably since it became part of the Fremont Street Experience.

ABOVE: Mary Wilson of the Supremes on stage at the Excalibur during the Supreme Slot Tourney in 1996.

RIGHT: The towers of Excalibur are at once majestic and ethereal. There are like Camelot with the dramatic lighting only Merlin could have imagined.

ABOVE: At the northeast corner of the Caesars Palace property, visitors are welcomed by the famous Quadriga statue, which includes four gold leaf horses and a charioteer.

LEFT: The Roman-Empire-themed Caesars Palace, opened on August 5, 1966 at the heart of the Strip, was one of the first great Las Vegas theme properties. The vast complex now includes a Planet Hollywood restaurant.

LEFT: Standing at the bustling center of the Strip, one is surrounded with landmarks. At the left is the north entrance to Caesars Palace, and in the middle distance is the marquee of the Mirage. The Imperial Palace is immediately across the Strip.

LEFT: The place where Tropicana Avenue crosses Las Vegas Boulevard South is known as the "Four Corner" section of the Strip. Two of these corners are home to the New York New York Hotel and Casino, and the great lion of the MGM Grand.

RIGHT: The Strip by night, looking north from Tropicana Avenue. Both the Mirage and Treasure Island are prominent in the distance. Because all the casinos are open 24 hours each day, the Strip remains a busy and vibrant place all night long.

LEFT: The future of Las Vegas can be seen in such developments as Steve Wynn's Bellagio. The design of the $1.3 billion resort hotel was inspired by the Italian village of Bellagio, which overlooks Lake Como. The Las Vegas Bellagio also has a lake, which will be home to a choreographed water ballet. The 3,000 guest rooms were deigned to make extensive use of imported marble.

INDEX

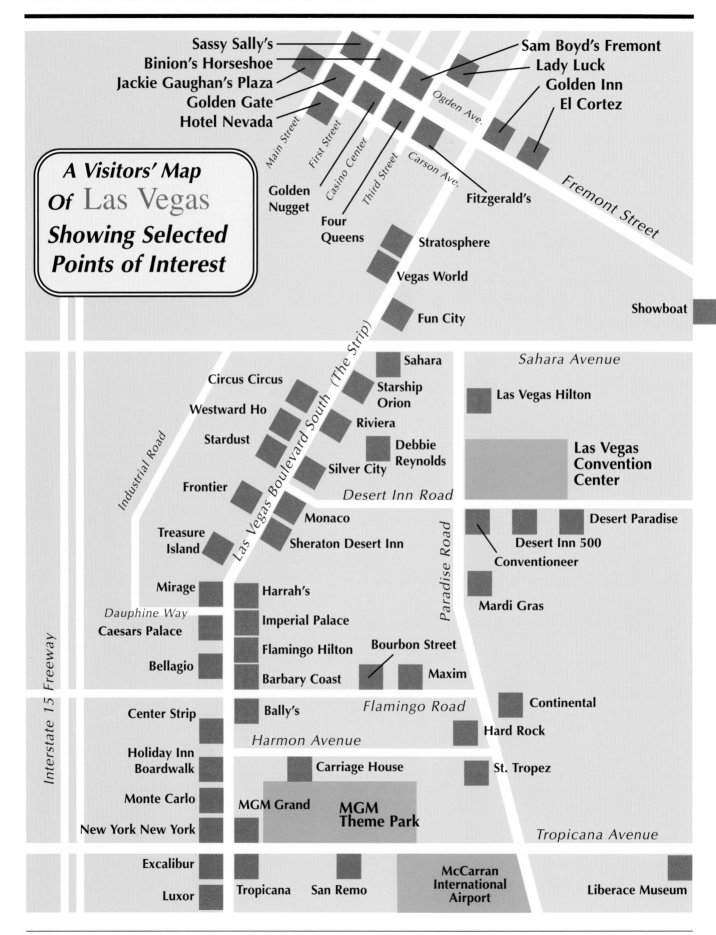

A Visitors' Map Of Las Vegas Showing Selected Points of Interest

Sassy Sally's
Binion's Horseshoe
Jackie Gaughan's Plaza
Golden Gate
Hotel Nevada

Sam Boyd's Fremont
Lady Luck
Golden Inn
El Cortez

Ogden Ave.

Main Street
First Street
Casino Center
Third Street
Carson Ave.

Fremont Street

Golden Nugget

Fitzgerald's

Four Queens

Stratosphere

Vegas World

Fun City

Showboat

Sahara Avenue

Circus Circus

Sahara

Starship Orion

Las Vegas Hilton

Westward Ho

Riviera

Stardust

Debbie Reynolds

Silver City

Las Vegas Convention Center

Frontier

Desert Inn Road

Industrial Road

Las Vegas Boulevard South (The Strip)

Monaco

Sheraton Desert Inn

Desert Paradise

Desert Inn 500

Conventioneer

Treasure Island

Paradise Road

Mirage

Harrah's

Mardi Gras

Dauphine Way

Caesars Palace

Imperial Palace

Bellagio

Flamingo Hilton

Bourbon Street

Barbary Coast

Maxim

Continental

Center Strip

Bally's

Flamingo Road

Interstate 15 Freeway

Harmon Avenue

Hard Rock

Holiday Inn Boardwalk

Carriage House

St. Tropez

Monte Carlo

MGM Grand

MGM Theme Park

New York New York

Tropicana Avenue

Excalibur

Luxor

Tropicana

San Remo

McCarran International Airport

Liberace Museum